QuoteOctopus.com

The best quotes

Publisher Contact

257 Swanston Street, Melbourne, VIC, AUSTRALIA

Email: hello@quoteoctopus.com

Social media: facebook.com/quoteoctopus

Acknowledgements

The team at Quote Octopus would like to thank our friends, family, suppliers and customers for making our vision of creating the highest-quality books a reality. Thanks for purchasing and enjoy the quotes!

This page is intentionally left blank

This page is intentionally left blank

Angry people are not beautiful.

Andie MacDowell

As I celebrate life, I can't help but think how young my mom was when she died of a heart attack at 53. My mom didn't get to meet her grandchildren, but I'm determined to watch mine grow up.

Andie MacDowell

As a proud spokesperson for L'Oreal Paris, I have communicated the 'Because You're Worth It' message many times, and know firsthand how empowering it is to say and how empowering it feels.

Andie MacDowell

As a single mother of four, my mother taught me that you always want to show up strong for the moments that really matter with family, friends, and community. I now recognize how her strength helped shape the person I am today and the mother that I have become.

Andie MacDowell

Because of technology today, we expect kids to stay in touch with us too much. I think that's unnatural. We really do have to give kids their freedom and allow them to go off and become adults.

Andie MacDowell

Being a model, you know, it's a short-lived vocation.

Andie MacDowell

Being prepared helps you feel more confident at the doctor's office. Think about what you want to ask and write those questions down.

Andie MacDowell

Diane Keaton was a big role model for me.

Andie MacDowell

Diane Keaton, I've worked with her as a director, and I think she's a really intelligent woman. I like the fact that the things that make her feel beautiful are more than just her face; it's who she is, and I live by that same theory. There are things I want to achieve in my life intellectually that make me feel beautiful.

Andie MacDowell

Divorce is horrible. I wouldn't wish that on my worst enemy. I don't think it's anything that's ever completely resolved.

Andie MacDowell

Do I really need to prove anything to anybody? I don't feel that I have to prove anything. The only thing that I have to prove is to myself, that I have value.

Andie MacDowell

Don't worry about the room being messy! Everything can't be perfect - you have to let some things go, and it's better to actually sit down on the floor with your child than spend time worrying about having a perfect house.

Andie MacDowell

During Katherine Hepburn's time when she was just coming into her own at 40.

Andie MacDowell

During my 40s, I thought I couldn't wear red lipstick. I thought it was just too much and I couldn't do it anymore. I don't know why. But now, I'm going to wear red lipstick for as long as I want.

Andie MacDowell

During my teen years, I was real emotional. I could be really up or down.

Andie MacDowell

Every woman goes through a lot of agony before she decides in favour of her own happiness or that of her children.

Andie MacDowell

Everybody perceives me because of my career that I'm a movie star, or I'm this model, but I'm still the same person I was when I was a little girl.

Andie MacDowell

For me, it's sad to say, but I would probably have a spiritual marriage but not a legal marriage, because I think so much about marriage starts to become about finances. It has nothing to do with God or feelings or the romantic side of marriage. It's about who owns what, who gets what? So what's the point?

Andie MacDowell

Having the option to be able to have a career and feel good about yourself as an individual and still be a great mother is definitely a possibility.

Andie MacDowell

Here's the thing with the business, is that when people like your work, and you make them money, you're set. When the critics like you, and you make the studios money, doors opened.

Andie MacDowell

How are we supposed to get old? What am I supposed to do? Am I supposed to get old? My kids tell me, 'We want you to look like a grandmother.' I agree with them. I want to look like a grandmother.

Andie MacDowell

How do I think the industry's changed? Films have changed a lot. I think women are finally able to get older and be sexy just like men. So I'm really enjoying that part - that's my evolution.

Andie MacDowell

I always say that kindness is the greatest beauty that you can have.

Andie MacDowell

I always think I look better after a yoga class. It's the same as a massage. We look so amazing after a massage because we're relaxed.

Andie MacDowell

I am an advocate for going to the doctor and going every year. I make sure that part of the checkup is spent talking about my heart with my doctor, and getting my numbers checked, and discussing the results. And I make sure that I understand the answers to my questions.

Andie MacDowell

I am committed to ovarian cancer research on a national level and in my community in the Carolinas. It is important to me to know the women that are true fighters of this difficult disease.

Andie MacDowell

I can usually tell when a woman is going through a divorce because they look so gaunt and tired and sad. It's just a huge sadness. It's horrible. It's like death. You mourn, but the person's still there.

Andie MacDowell

I can't see as well as I used to. Which is actually convenient because everything I see is in extremely soft focus! I think that's God's little gift to me.

Andie MacDowell

I did three movies in a row, and that was horrible. It was a horrible experience for me.

Andie MacDowell

I don't know that anyone comes from a truly functional family.

Andie MacDowell

I don't pass judgment on anybody, but personally, I prefer a more natural look. I think it's helping my longevity in my career because I'm playing my age.

Andie MacDowell

I don't think that youth should be glorified.

Andie MacDowell

I don't want to be agitated so much on television. I don't need to watch any more agitation.

Andie MacDowell

I eat an enormous amount of fruits and vegetables.

Andie MacDowell

I eat healthy, but that doesn't mean I don't enjoy myself. I eat ice cream and chocolate, as my metabolism is pretty fast because I work out so much.

Andie MacDowell

I exercise every day. It's what makes me happy.

Andie MacDowell

I feel like I've had so many successes on so many levels, even if it is just my relationships with my friends.

Andie MacDowell

I feel really good about the things I've accomplished in my life, and I don't want to look younger.

Andie MacDowell

I had a whole bunch of very successful movies. I have worked with some incredible people - incredible.

Andie MacDowell

I hate auditions.

Andie MacDowell

I like being a part of something. I like participating and being part of a group.

Andie MacDowell

I like to work out every day. I run, walk, do machines. I'm not neurotic about food. My rule is, don't let yourself get over a certain weight. If you gain 5lb, stop before it gets worse.

Andie MacDowell

I like what L'Oreal stands for, which is women of worth.

Andie MacDowell

I lived in Paris when I was 20 and 21, and actually knew people that worked for the government there, that talked about terrorism in the country 20 years ago.

Andie MacDowell

I love 'Forrest Gump;' I like sweet, cheery, happy movies. But it has some dark moments too.

Andie MacDowell

I love being an advocate for women as we get older so that we can feel comfortable with ourselves. It's all about being healthy for me now.

Andie MacDowell

I love being an advocate for women as we get older so that we can feel comfortable with ourselves.

Andie MacDowell

I love learning, and I think that curiosity is a wonderful gift.

Andie MacDowell

I love the idea of living a life that is completely humble and quiet.

Andie MacDowell

I loved dancing as a young girl.

Andie MacDowell

I make an enormous amount of salads, but my salads are like meals. They're amazing. I like going down to the farmers' market and looking to see whatever you can find, because you can put anything in a salad.

Andie MacDowell

I need some downtime before I go to sleep.

Andie MacDowell

I never 'shunned' L.A., like people say. And I do think you can raise children well there, but it's definitely harder.

Andie MacDowell

I never dye my own hair, I don't know if I could get every spot, and I have a good bit of grey.

Andie MacDowell

I play games on-set at work. Sometimes I can't remember people's names, so I start throwing out clues. Like if I can't think of George Clooney, I'll say, 'You know, drop-dead gorgeous, was on a big TV show... ' Until someone says his name, I can't finish my story!

Andie MacDowell

I realize that I'm in the top one percent of the world. I've traveled a lot. I've seen immense poverty in the world, and I can't live with everything I've had and be comfortable with everything I have unless I do something for the rest of the world.

Andie MacDowell

I remember early on, in my very, very early days, I had a makeup artist tell me that I needed to get an attitude. I had no idea what he was talking about.

Andie MacDowell

I remember tap-dancing and singing in front of the TV when I was a kid, telling my dad to stop watching Ed Sullivan or Milton Berle and watch me.

Andie MacDowell

I remember what I was like as a teenager, with an enormous amount of energy and hormones. You have to be able to release it, and dancing is really an innocent way.

Andie MacDowell

I remember when Meryl Streep did an ad for American Express, the press harassed her.

Andie MacDowell

I still love finding the soul of the characters I play and defining who they are. This to me is my paint set, and the colors are always exciting to choose.

Andie MacDowell

I think a lot of times people who jump from one movie to another don't enjoy their private life. It's a great way to escape reality. But I enjoy my life.

Andie MacDowell

I think every time in your life is valuable, and you need to exist in that moment. Because if you don't - you lose it.

Andie MacDowell

I think hidden underneath a lot of teachers are very sexy women.

Andie MacDowell

I think role models exist, but they usually don't get the light because people like scandal.

Andie MacDowell

I think sometimes I intimidate people. I've been told that. But I feel I'm the least intimidating person possible.

Andie MacDowell

I think sometimes we seem to obsess on negativity.

Andie MacDowell

I think the human body is beautiful, and I don't really have a huge problem in dealing with it, but it's the context, the environment and what I feel about it that that makes the difference for me.

Andie MacDowell

I think there is sexy. And then there's tacky sexy. When you're young, you can get away with tacky sexy. I mean, it's not even tacky when you're young. But when you get older, it's just tacky.

Andie MacDowell

I think women have an innate ability to be intuitive with people that they truly love, but they have to trust that inner voice, and I think it is there. I think we are more intuitive than men.

Andie MacDowell

I think yoga has given me better posture. People don't realise how strong it makes you. You have to use your body weight to hold yourself. As you get older, you're supposed to lift weights, but I find that kind of boring. Yoga is lifting my own body.

Andie MacDowell

I tried to do things independently with each child.

Andie MacDowell

I tried to tell them about the dating process because I'm single now and how horrible it is and how many foolish experiences I had had dating. So I was really selling him hard, but the whole time he really wanted me!

Andie MacDowell

I try really hard not to be attached to success.

Andie MacDowell

I want to be able to speak every language. If I could have any talent and I get to choose it, and be naturally gifted and speak every language. It's not going to happen, but it sure would be nice. It's a good wish.

Andie MacDowell

I want to play some really good, interesting, crazy characters. I want to take some chances. I want to take risks. I want to have fun and just keep working. That's all I really care about.

Andie MacDowell

I was a hard rocker when I was in high school.

Andie MacDowell

I was fortunate to be able to do two movies with Harold Ramis. He was the kindest of any director with whom I worked. Harold was a genius. On top of his talent, he could do the 'New York Times' crossword puzzle faster than anyone! I am lucky to have known him as well as I did. I will miss him.

Andie MacDowell

I was from a little rinky-dink town - to be a model... it looked like a lot of fun. I'd look at the girls, and they always looked happy.

Andie MacDowell

I was six when my parents divorced, and that was tough for me.

Andie MacDowell

I will do simple cleanses and have a day where I'm quiet and don't talk. I need to have this experience, especially after work has been really intense.

Andie MacDowell

I willingly devoted myself to my children and to my husband. I come from a broken home, and I decided a long time ago that I would put my family ahead of everything.

Andie MacDowell

I wish there was a news channel that really told you what was going on in the world, not just sensationalized news.

Andie MacDowell

I wouldn't wear really short dresses anymore - just don't feel comfortable in them.

Andie MacDowell

I'm a huge Muppets fan. Gigantic. I think they're genius. I think they're some of the best work out there and completely underrated, just because of how genius they are. I love that kind of humor. It's so innocent but brilliant.

Andie MacDowell

I'm actually a pretty clean-cut person.

Andie MacDowell

I'm always reading several books at the same time, depending on how deeply engrossed in it I am, if it's fiction and if it captures me.

Andie MacDowell

I'm an artist, but, as I get older, I really want to do philanthropic work and help people.

Andie MacDowell

I'm comfortable in front of a camera, and I'm used to being watched, although that kind of bugged me at first. On the stage, though, I'm scared. I really get frightened in front of people.

Andie MacDowell

I'm just human, and I have great relationships with the people that work for me.

Andie MacDowell

I'm not a huge TV person. I don't like having the noise when I'm doing other things unless I'm really lonely, and then I turn the TV on. But I do like to sit down and watch TV in the evenings.

Andie MacDowell

I'm not a party person. I'm a nerd. I'm not an extrovert in that way at all. The things I enjoy doing could be boring to somebody else.

Andie MacDowell

I'm not aiming for an Academy Award.

Andie MacDowell

I'm really addicted to water. I carry a bottle of water everywhere I go. I know people think I'm a nut.

Andie MacDowell

I'm really not techno-savvy - that's just not my personality.

Andie MacDowell

I'm sorry, but in my generation and where I came from, only sailors got tattoos. Not ladies.

Andie MacDowell

I'm strong. I'm outspoken. I feel like I'm equal to men. I can walk in the woods just as much and as far as a man can. Yet I'm still female. I'm very female.

Andie MacDowell

I've already made a substantial commitment to wildlife by putting my land in the easement. It won't be developed. It will remain there in perpetuity - will be there for the wildlife.

Andie MacDowell

I've always been a very active person.

Andie MacDowell

I've been a Christian for a long time, and I think that Christianity gets a bad rap. I think that people's perception of what a Christian is today is something that is close-minded and narrow, and that's not what I am.

Andie MacDowell

I've been practicing Ayurvedic medicine, and I've read the 'Bhagavad Gita' and Rumi, and these are very important.

Andie MacDowell

I've had some really big hits with 'Groundhog Day' and 'Michael,' 'Multiplicity,' 'Four Weddings and a Funeral.'

Andie MacDowell

I've heard that George Clooney did something like nine pilots before 'ER' was picked up, way back when he was doing TV. It's just the way the business works. There are a lot of pilots that we've never seen. It's protocol.

Andie MacDowell

I've worked with producers who have told me to lose weight, and I'm not overweight, but they want you to look strange, anorexic, horrible. It's odd. It's like they are exerting a power over women, that they want them to look really frail.

Andie MacDowell

In 1984, I starred in 'Greystoke: The Legend Of Tarzan,' my first movie. My lines ended up being dubbed by Glenn Close, supposedly because my accent was 'too southern'. It was completely humiliating at the time. I became a laughing stock. I'm amazed that I managed to pick myself up and dust myself off.

Andie MacDowell

In modeling, because you're the center of attention, it builds up people's egos. Sometimes people lose touch with reality. But that happens with acting, too.

Andie MacDowell

In the days when I used to tweet, I would encounter comments wishing death upon me. There were people who claimed they were sticking pins in my effigy because they couldn't stand me. There's some seriously disturbed people out there.

Andie MacDowell

It kind of cracks me up when people say I'm hot because I just think that that's a term that I don't have to deal with anymore.

Andie MacDowell

It's interesting now; with social media, you are actually interacting with fans.

Andie MacDowell

It's so funny to get a call from Dustin Hoffman because he has that great voice.

Andie MacDowell

Kindness can come from someone on Twitter, it can come from someone on the street, it can come from someone at work. Without kindness, I don't know what I would do. The greatest part of life is the simple things.

Andie MacDowell

Like anybody, you have moments when you question yourself and you're insecure.

Andie MacDowell

Looking back, I realise I had to grow up and be responsible at a very tender age.

Andie MacDowell

My biggest regret is rolling in regret. It is best to pick yourself up , dust yourself off and move on.

Andie MacDowell

My children without a doubt are my greatest accomplishment. If I did nothing else I would feel just having and raising them would be enough. The rest is icing.

Andie MacDowell

My favourite thing is to be somebody else, no longer be me.

Andie MacDowell

My girls have been a great support to me. I come to them when I need to make a decision; they love to watch me work.

Andie MacDowell

My high school experience was kind of like 'Mean Girls.' It was very much like a bad B movie. 'This is where the jocks sit, and this is where the cheerleaders sit.' And I never really fit in. I guess I was sort of a theatre geek, but the activity that I was most invested in was speech and debate.

Andie MacDowell

My kids learned to be independent.

Andie MacDowell

My mother and I used to watch 'Maude,' and I think she loved 'Maude' because my mother wanted to see strong women out there with a voice.

Andie MacDowell

My mother and grandmother both had beautiful skin.

Andie MacDowell

North Carolina has been so great because nobody asks me about work.

Andie MacDowell

Not many college students know what they want to do.

Andie MacDowell

Oh, all southern women say they're sorry. You could do almost anything, bump into some one, don't spread the jam right, you're always sorry. I've had people tell me to stop saying it so much!

Andie MacDowell

One of the reasons I didn't really want to do TV earlier in my career was because it is so life-consuming, and I wanted to spend time with my kids and be a mother.

Andie MacDowell

People that are 40, they don't sit around at talk about gray hair and how it covers their hair. They talk about highlighting, of course they're covering gray, but they don't talk about it that way. They're going to get their colors because they need a little lightening.

Andie MacDowell

Pregnancy changed my body; it changed the way I walk.

Andie MacDowell

Sexiness comes with maturity.

Andie MacDowell

Some women are naturally thin. But there needs to be an appreciation for a variety of types of women because we don't all come in one package. We're not pre-destined to all be a size six. It's very hard for a large group of women to maintain a thinness which is, after all, only natural to a few people.

Andie MacDowell

Some women are naturally thin. But there needs to be an appreciation for a variety of types of women because we don't all come in one package. We're not pre-destined to all be a size six.

Andie MacDowell

Someday, I'll make a movie with a British accent.

Andie MacDowell

Sometimes I get intimidated by people, intellectuals, because I don't have a great education. The only thing I feel helps me compete with all these people, people with degrees from Harvard, that you're thrown in with and have to work with, is that I'm grounded.

Andie MacDowell

The problem with my mother is that she didn't go to the doctor. And I think by the time she started to show symptoms that something might not be right, and finally went to the doctor, she was so close to her death that she couldn't get the care she had needed. Her big issue was not going to the doctor.

Andie MacDowell

The riskiest thing I have done in my fifties is to do a Polish accent for a new film. I had a great time working on it and two wonderful people to guide me. A dialect coach that I have known for thirty years and a Polish actor.

Andie MacDowell

The thing is, we live in a contemporary world, and being able to make yourself the best person you can possible be can be difficult. But as long as you're trying to figure it out, and you're really looking in the right direction, everything's going to be all right.

Andie MacDowell

The truth is that humans have the potential to be horrific. And I think being conscious of that is important.

Andie MacDowell

There are loads of actresses that modelled. They just weren't famous. There weren't a lot that were really known as models that became actresses, but there are hordes of them that did modelling before such as Anjelica Huston, Jessica Lange, Sharon Stone, Demi Moore and Geena Davis. There are loads of 'em.

Andie MacDowell

There are lots of great actresses who are great because they'll do anything.

Andie MacDowell

There is a comfortable feeling in small towns. It is salubrious.

Andie MacDowell

There's a deep piece of me that wants to be very personal and not share everything with everybody and not put it out there.

Andie MacDowell

We can sit around and go, okay, is there really a plan, does somebody really know what's happening, is it all planned out, because sometimes it just seems too remarkable to me the things that have happened to me.

Andie MacDowell

We don't need any more reality TV, women yelling at each other. I can't watch that stuff.

Andie MacDowell

We've become such a multitasking society that just paying attention to the road doesn't seem to be that important anymore. I have to remind my kids all the time that that's what you're supposed to be doing in the car.

Andie MacDowell

When I modeled, I lived in Europe and worked all the time. I did runway, and that's all I did.

Andie MacDowell

When my mother had four girls, and she could tell her marriage was falling apart, she went back to college and got her degree in music and education.

Andie MacDowell

When the children were little, I'd fly into L.A. for a specific work project, but then I'd leave again, and when I was home, I wouldn't even read a script.

Andie MacDowell

When you are authentic, you create a certain energy... people want to be around you because you are unique.

Andie MacDowell

When your kids are their hungriest, put out raw vegetables and dip - simple. It takes two seconds.

Andie MacDowell

Where I live, the majority of men are married to women their own age.

Andie MacDowell

Who's to say I can't find some great work when I'm 55 or 65?

Andie MacDowell

With all that's going on in our lives and the world, reducing stress is important, and it's a factor in heart health.

Andie MacDowell

Women who make the choice to have grey hair - I think that's beautiful.

Andie MacDowell

Wonderful things happen when you turn 50: you change perspective. You ask, 'Who am I? What do I want to do with my life? What have I not done that I want to do?'

Andie MacDowell

You know what may be the oddest thing about being a star? Stars have an effect on people. It's a responsibility, and it's frightening.

Andie MacDowell

You've got to take the hems down, especially past 50. I don't care how good your legs are.

Andie MacDowell